THINK LIKE YOUR DOG

Understanding Behaviour Through Stress, Emotion and Real Life

AMY CURRAN

Copyright © 2026 Amy Curran All rights reserved.

No part of this book may be reproduced, stored in a retrieval system, or transmitted in any form or by any means - electronic, mechanical, photocopying, recording, or otherwise - without the prior written permission of the author, except for brief quotations used in reviews or educational contexts.

Think Like Your Dog: Understanding Behaviour Through Stress, Emotion and Real Life

Text copyright © 2026 Amy Curran
Illustrations copyright © 2026 Amy Curran
Cover photograph © Byron Illyes

Audiobook read by Sonia Hardie

ISBN (Paperback): 978-0-6455623-4-7
ISBN (Hardcover): 978-1-7645031-0-5
ISBN (eBook): 978-0-6455623-5-4
ISBN (Audiobook): 978-0-6455623-6-1

First Edition
First published 2026

The information in this book is provided for educational and informational purposes only. While every effort has been made to ensure accuracy, the author makes no guarantees regarding individual outcomes. Animal behaviour is influenced by many variables, including environment, history, health, and context.

This book is not a substitute for professional veterinary, behavioural, or medical advice. Readers are encouraged to seek appropriate professional support where safety or wellbeing is a concern.

Printed in Australia.

For Bernie,

*Thank you for teaching me to slow down, truly listen, and notice what others overlook.
You lay beside me as I wrote this book, and I promised you I would carry your lessons into the world - so other dogs could be heard too.*

"A good dog doesn't just change your life - they change the way you see everything else."

THINK LIKE YOUR DOG

Understanding Behaviour Through Stress, Emotion and Real Life

CONTENTS

Author's Note 7

Introduction 9

    Orientation 13

    What This Book Is - and What It Is Not 15

Bernie **17**

Part I: Understanding Behaviour **25**

    Chapter 1: Behaviour is Communication 27

    Chapter 2: Stress - The Invisible Driver 39

    Chapter 3: Tolerance Is Not The Same As Calm 51

Part II: Why Behaviour Escalates **61**

    Chapter 4: Why Punishment Fails Dogs 63

    Chapter 5: The Nervous System Comes First 71

    Chapter 6: Environment Matters More Than You Think
.... 81

Part III: Life, Ethics & Responsibility 91
    Chapter 7: When Life Changes, Dogs Change 93
    Chapter 8: Multi-Dog Homes & Social Pressure 105
    Chapter 9: Choice, Consent & Safety 115

Part IV: Action & Support 125
    Chapter 10: What Helping Actually Looks Like 127
    Chapter 11: When To Ask For Help 137

Conclusion: Listening Changes Everything 145

Acknowledgements 149

About The Author 153

Author's Note

This book was written slowly, deliberately, and with great care.

Not because dogs are complicated - but because the way we talk about their behaviour often is.

Over many years of working with dogs and the people who love them, I began to notice a pattern. Not in the dogs, but in the conversations around them. So many owners arrived feeling anxious, defeated, or ashamed - convinced they were doing something wrong, or that their dog was "difficult," "dominant," or broken in some way.

What I saw instead were dogs responding to stress, pressure, environment, and change - often in very understandable ways.

I wrote this book to create space for a different kind of conversation. One that doesn't rely on blame or urgency. One that replaces labels with understanding, and quick fixes with perspective. One that allows both dogs and people to breathe.

This is not a book about control.
It is a book about context.
It is not a book about obedience.
It is a book about communication.

If at any point while reading you feel recognised, relieved, or reassured, then this book is doing what it was meant to do.

Introduction

If you're holding this book, there's a good chance you care deeply about your dog. You may also be worried.

Perhaps your dog has begun behaving in ways you don't understand. Maybe they've always been sensitive, reactive, or easily overwhelmed, and you've been told - directly or indirectly - that you should be handling things better by now. Or perhaps nothing dramatic has happened at all, but something feels *off*, and you can't quite explain why.

This book is for you.

Think Like Your Dog is not about teaching dogs to fit neatly into our expectations. It's about learning to see the world from their side - to understand how stress, emotion, environment, and lived experience shape behaviour long before a problem appears.

Because dogs don't experience life the way we do. They don't have context, long-term reasoning, or the ability to explain themselves with words. What they do have is a nervous system that responds constantly to safety, pressure, predictability, and change. Their behaviour is the outward expression of how well, or how poorly, they are coping in that moment.

Behaviour is not attitude. It is information.

This book is not a training manual filled with commands, drills, or techniques designed to force behaviour into place. It won't tell you how to dominate your dog, suppress communication, or demand compliance at any cost.

Instead, it invites you to slow down.

To notice patterns rather than react to moments.
To consider their stress before discipline.
To recognise tolerance before it collapses.
To understand behaviour in the context of real life - not ideal situations.

Throughout this book, we'll explore how behaviour is shaped by emotional load, environmental pressure, nervous system capacity, and change over time. We'll look at why calm is often mistaken for compliance, why punishment fails to create lasting safety, and why understanding context matters more than any single method.

We'll also talk honestly about responsibility, ethics, consent, and safety - without blame, urgency, or judgement.

Thinking like your dog doesn't mean excusing unsafe behaviour or lowering standards. It means making better decisions earlier. It means recognising when a dog is coping and when they are quietly struggling. And it means understanding that most behaviour does not come out of nowhere - it builds, often silently, over time.

This book isn't about doing more. Often, it's about doing less - with intention.

You don't need to be perfect to help your dog. You don't need to get everything right. You just need curiosity, observation, and a willingness to listen - even when what you're seeing challenges what you've been taught.

If this book helps you see your dog more clearly, feel more confident in your decisions, and replace frustration with understanding, then it has done exactly what it was written to do.

Orientation

This book is not designed to be rushed.

You don't need to read it in one sitting, and you don't need to agree with every sentence to benefit from it. Many readers will find themselves pausing often - reflecting on moments, behaviours, or decisions they've seen before but are now viewing differently. That's intentional.

Each chapter builds on the last, but they are also written to stand alone. You may recognise situations immediately, or you may not see their relevance until later. Both experiences are valid.

Some chapters will feel practical. Others may feel confronting. Some may simply put words to things you've sensed but never articulated.

You don't need to "apply" everything in this book. The aim is not to create more pressure, but to create clarity. Behaviour change rarely begins with action - it begins with understanding.

If at any point you feel defensive, uncomfortable, or uncertain, pause. Those moments are often signals that an assumption is being challenged, not that you are doing something wrong.

This book is not asking you to become perfect, stricter, or more in control. It is asking you to become more observant, more thoughtful, and more willing to consider behaviour in context.

Read with curiosity. Return to chapters as needed. Let understanding develop over time.

Thinking like your dog is not a destination - it's a practice.

What This Book Is - and What It Is Not

What this book *is*

This book is:

- a reframing of behaviour through the lens of nervous systems
- an invitation to slow down and reduce pressure
- grounded in observation, context, and lived experience
- supportive of safety, realism, and sustainability
- written for people who want to understand, not control

It is designed to help behaviour make sense - even when it doesn't change.

What this book *is not*

This book is not:

- a training manual
- a set of techniques or protocols
- a promise of quick results
- a replacement for professional, in-person support
- a judgement on how you've handled things so far

It will not tell you how to stop behaviours. It will not ask dogs to push through discomfort. It will not suggest that understanding alone replaces safety.

What it offers instead is a different starting point - one that prioritises nervous systems, context, and care.

Bernie

Bernie is a big dog.

Not just tall or heavy - big in presence, big in feelings, big in how he experiences the world. He's a performer by nature. You can't look at him without smiling. He's full of life and optimism, with an energy that often feels bigger than his own body.

However, that energy doesn't last long. It flares brightly, then fades just as quickly. But in those moments, it fills the space around him.

Not all dogs understand it the way he means it.

When Bernie approaches, his size and enthusiasm arrive before his intent. Many dogs who meet him are already on the defensive - not because he's aggressive, but because he's overwhelming. Their reactions are almost always rooted in fear. Growls. Snaps. Warnings.

Bernie is always left confused.

He doesn't understand that he's frightened them. His tail keeps wagging. His body stays open. He remains full of hope, even when the message coming back is anything but welcoming.

For his own protection, Bernie is never off lead around other dogs. He has been snapped at. He has been growled at. And still, he shows up believing this time might be different.

For a long time, I wanted to fix that.

I wanted him to make friends. To be calmer. Easier. Less much. I wanted him to move through the world in a way that felt more comfortable - not just for him, but for everyone else too. I felt responsible for how he was perceived. I carried the weight of his size and intensity, and the pressure to make him different.

I told myself it was for his own good. But what I was really doing was asking Bernie to shrink himself to fit a world that hadn't made room for him.

Because when dogs are given the time to see him properly, everything changes.

Once other dogs get past that first moment - once they realise he is kind, gentle, and emotionally honest - they love him for life. Bernie lives peacefully with all of our cats. He has even helped me raise a singleton cattle dog puppy, patiently teaching boundaries, play, and calm in a way no human ever could.

Bernie isn't rough. He isn't dominant. He isn't unaware. He is just intense - and intensity, without context, is often misunderstood.

Bernie is also far from unintelligent. He is the first Bernese Mountain Dog in the world to achieve the highest level of Animal Actor Accreditation with the Animal Actors Académie Internationale (AAAI), the global certifying body for animals working in film and television. He has appeared in television commercials, billboards, and catalogues - calm, focused, and reliable. On set, he has always been impeccable. Surrounded by lights, people, equipment, and noise, he regulated himself with ease, his attention anchored steadily on me.

Which made the contrast harder to explain.

Because everywhere else - in ordinary, everyday dog spaces - I found myself hoping no one recognised me as a dog trainer.

Bernie wasn't unfocused. He wasn't untrained. He wasn't incapable of self-control. He had already shown, repeatedly, that he could regulate beautifully when the environment was structured, predictable, and safe.

That contradiction mattered.

It told me his reactions around other dogs weren't about skill or intelligence. They were about context, emotion, and nervous system load.

Bernie's size meant other dogs noticed him immediately. His hopeful, forward energy arrived quickly, before other dogs had time to gather information. To dogs who were already cautious, guarded, or carrying their own stress, that combination felt like too much, too soon.

Their fear made sense.

Bernie's communication style is honest, but it isn't subtle. He doesn't hedge or posture. He doesn't mask. Dogs who rely on distance, strategy, or caution often responded with warnings because they needed space and didn't know how else to ask for it quickly enough.

Bernie, meanwhile, didn't read those responses as rejection. He stayed open. His optimism overrode his caution. Even after negative encounters, he continued to approach the world with hope.

What looked like a behaviour problem was really a mismatch.

The pressure of first meetings. The lack of space. The speed at which expectations were placed on him. The accumulation of social stress layered on top of previous experiences.

Bernie wasn't misbehaving. He wasn't ignoring cues. He wasn't failing to learn. He was communicating - constantly - and I wasn't listening properly yet.

The shift didn't come from a technique or a breakthrough moment. It came from a question that landed softly and refused to leave.

What if I stop trying to change him, and change the world around him instead?

That question changed everything.

I didn't need to make Bernie smaller.

I needed to lessen the intensity of first meetings so other dogs could meet him with curiosity instead of fear. I needed to slow things down, create distance, and remove social pressure before asking him to engage.

I needed to help him be calm - not by suppressing who he was, but by supporting him to feel safe enough to soften.

When I stopped correcting Bernie and started observing him, the story looked different. His enthusiasm wasn't recklessness - it was hope. His intensity wasn't disobedience - it was honesty. His struggles weren't flaws - they were signals.

I didn't make Bernie calmer.

I made his world kinder.

I adjusted expectations. I adjusted environments. I adjusted how much pressure I put on both of us.

And something remarkable happened.

Bernie softened - not because he was controlled, but because he felt safer. He became more regulated - not because he was managed, but because he was understood. He didn't turn into a different dog. He became more himself.

That was the moment this book began, even though I didn't know it yet.

Bernie didn't teach me how to train dogs.

He taught me how to listen.

Everything that follows comes from that place.

Part I: Understanding Behaviour

Before we can change behaviour, we need to understand it.

This section explores behaviour not as a problem to be fixed, but as information shaped by stress, emotion, and nervous system capacity. These chapters lay the foundation for everything that follows - because without understanding why behaviour exists, attempts to change it often miss the mark.

Chapter 1:
Behaviour is Communication

When a dog growls, hides, lunges, barks, freezes, or refuses to cooperate, the word most often used is *difficult*.

Difficult dog.
Difficult behaviour.
Difficult phase.

It is a word that carries judgement, frustration, and often a quiet sense of failure. It suggests that the dog is being deliberately challenging, stubborn, or oppositional - that they know better and are choosing not to comply.

But dogs are not being difficult.

They are communicating.

Dogs do not have language in the way humans do. They cannot explain that they are overwhelmed, frightened, confused, grieving, overstimulated, or unsure. They cannot tell us that something feels unsafe, unpredictable, or too much. Instead, they rely on the only tools available to them: their bodies, their behaviour, and their nervous systems.

Behaviour is not attitude.
Behaviour is information.

Every behaviour a dog offers exists for a reason. It serves a function. It is an attempt to cope with the world as the dog experiences it in that moment. Sometimes that attempt looks calm and socially acceptable. Sometimes it does not. But even the behaviours we find most confronting are still communication.

A growl is not defiance. It is a warning.
Avoidance is not stubbornness. It is self-protection.
Escalation is not dominance. It is desperation.

Most dogs do not want conflict. They do not seek to challenge humans or control situations. They want safety, predictability, and relief from pressure. When those needs are met, behaviour tends to soften naturally. When they are not, behaviour intensifies - not because the dog is trying to be problematic, but because communication has failed.

How behaviour gets misunderstood

Many dog owners come to behaviour support already carrying shame.

They say things like:
"He knows better."
"She's doing it for attention."
"He's trying to test me."
"She's fine most of the time - until she isn't."

These phrases all assume intent. They suggest that the dog is making a calculated choice to misbehave.

But dogs do not operate from spite, manipulation, or moral reasoning. They do not weigh up consequences in the way humans do. They operate from emotional state, learning history, environmental pressure, and nervous system capacity.

When behaviour is misunderstood, responses often escalate:

- fear is punished
- communication is suppressed
- warning signs are ignored
- pressure increases

And then, when behaviour finally becomes unavoidable - when a growl turns into a snap, or avoidance turns into aggression - it feels sudden and shocking.

In reality, it almost never is.

Behaviour rarely comes out of nowhere

One of the most dangerous myths in dog ownership is the idea that stress and discomfort are obvious.

They often aren't.

Dogs communicate long before behaviour escalates, but their early signals are subtle. They are easy to miss, especially in busy homes or environments where dogs are expected to cope quietly.

Early communication often looks like:

- lip licking
- yawning outside of tiredness
- turning the head away
- brief stiffening
- slowing down

- leaving the room
- avoiding eye contact

These signals are frequently dismissed or misunderstood. They are quiet. They don't disrupt the household. They don't demand immediate action. As a result, they go unaddressed.

Over time, pressure builds.

When subtle communication fails, dogs escalate - not because they want to, but because they have learned that earlier signals did not work.

Behaviour that feels "out of character" is often the final attempt to be heard.

Why labelling behaviour is risky

Labels are convenient. They give us a sense of certainty and control.

Reactive.
Aggressive.
Anxious.
Dominant.

But labels can obscure more than they reveal.

When we label a dog, we often stop asking *why*. We stop looking at context, triggers, environment, and emotional state. We treat behaviour as a fixed trait rather than a response.

A dog who growls in one context may be calm and relaxed in another. A dog who avoids handling may be confident and playful when given choice. Behaviour shifts when circumstances shift.

Dogs are not static. Their behaviour reflects what they are experiencing - not who they are.

Communication is a safety system

From a safety perspective, behaviour is invaluable information.

A dog who growls is saying, "I am uncomfortable. Please create distance."
A dog who avoids is saying, "This feels unsafe."
A dog who freezes is saying, "I don't know how to cope right now."

These signals allow humans to intervene early - to adjust the environment, reduce pressure, or remove the dog from a situation before escalation occurs.

When communication is respected, dogs rarely need to escalate further.

When communication is punished or ignored, dogs learn that warning signals are ineffective or unsafe. The next time, they may skip them entirely.

This is how dogs become "unpredictable." Not because they lack warning, but because warning has been silenced.

The cost of not listening

When behaviour is treated as a problem to be stopped rather than a message to be understood, several things happen:

- stress increases rather than resolves
- trust erodes
- coping strategies collapse
- risk escalates

Owners often feel trapped between conflicting advice - some telling them to be firmer, others telling them to ignore behaviour, others insisting the dog will "get over it."

What is rarely explained clearly is this: **behaviour will continue until the underlying need is addressed.**

Stopping behaviour without addressing the cause does not create calm. It creates suppression.

Suppressed behaviour does not disappear. It resurfaces - often in more intense and dangerous forms.

A different way of seeing your dog

The most powerful shift an owner can make is not a new technique or command. It is a change in perspective.

Instead of asking:
"How do I stop this behaviour?"

Ask:
"What is my dog trying to tell me right now?"

That question invites curiosity instead of frustration. It opens the door to understanding patterns, triggers, and pressure points. It allows owners to respond earlier - before behaviour escalates into something frightening or unsafe.

Listening to behaviour does not mean excusing it. It means interpreting it correctly so that effective, humane action can follow.

> **A REAL LIFE MOMENT**
>
> *A dog was described as "very calm in public."*
>
> *He lay down quietly at cafés, stayed in place during social gatherings, and rarely made a sound. People often commented on how well trained he was. His guardian felt proud - and relieved - that he seemed to cope so well. At home, however, things were different.*
>
> *After outings, the dog paced, startled easily, and reacted sharply to small disturbances. He struggled to settle and became irritable in situations that had never been a problem before. The contrast was confusing. How could a dog who appeared so calm outside be so unsettled later?*
>
> *The answer wasn't disobedience or inconsistency. Outside, the dog was tolerating intense sensory and social pressure. He was holding himself still, suppressing movement, and staying hyper-aware of his surroundings. What looked like calm was effort.*

At home - where his nervous system finally had permission to release that effort - the cost became visible.

When expectations around public outings were softened, the focus shifted away from what the dog should tolerate and toward what he could realistically cope with. Walks became shorter and less frequent, busy environments were avoided, and outings were no longer treated as something he had to "get through." If he showed signs of stress early, the outing ended rather than being pushed to completion.

Recovery was also prioritised. After unavoidable exposure to stimulation, the dog was given time and space to decompress - quiet rest at home, predictable routines, and reduced demands rather than more activity layered on top. There was no attempt to train calm into him in those moments, no insistence that he "settle" before he was ready.

As the overall load on his nervous system decreased, his behaviour at home began to change.

Not because he had been trained to be calmer, but because he no longer had to endure quite so much beforehand.

Behaviour makes sense in context

When behaviour is viewed in isolation, it feels chaotic and unpredictable.

When behaviour is viewed in context - emotional state, environment, recent stress, physical comfort, routine - it almost always makes sense.

Dogs are not unpredictable.
They are responsive.

And once you begin to see behaviour as communication, the dog in front of you starts to feel less confusing - and far more understandable.

Looking ahead

In the next chapter, we will explore stress - the invisible force driving so much behaviour - and why understanding stress is essential if we want to create lasting change rather than temporary compliance.

Behaviour is the language dogs use to survive in a human world.

When we learn to listen, everything that follows becomes clearer.

Chapter 2:
Stress - The Invisible Driver

Stress is the force behind many behaviours that worry, frustrate, or confuse dog owners - yet it is one of the least understood elements of behaviour.

When people think of stress, they often imagine extremes: panic, trembling, obvious fear, or frantic escape attempts. But stress does not need to be dramatic to be powerful. In fact, the most influential stress is often the kind that goes unnoticed.

Stress works quietly. It accumulates over time, lowers tolerance, and reshapes how dogs experience the world. When behaviour changes "suddenly," stress has usually been present for far longer than anyone realised.

To understand behaviour, we must understand stress.

What stress really is

Stress is the body's response to anything that challenges a dog's sense of safety, predictability, or control. It is not inherently bad. In short bursts, stress is adaptive. It allows dogs to react quickly, avoid danger, and cope with new situations.

The problem arises when stress becomes **chronic, stacked,** or **inescapable**.

Dogs experience stress through a wide range of everyday situations, including:

- unfamiliar environments
- unpredictable routines
- social pressure
- lack of choice
- emotional tension in the household
- physical discomfort or pain
- repeated exposure to things they find overwhelming

What matters is not whether we think something should be stressful, but whether the dog experiences it as such. Stress is subjective. Two dogs can experience the same environment very differently

Acute stress and chronic stress

Acute stress is short-lived. It might occur during a loud noise, a sudden surprise, or a brief moment of fear. When dogs are supported and allowed to recover, acute stress often resolves without lasting impact.

Chronic stress is different.

Chronic stress occurs when dogs are exposed to pressure without adequate recovery. This may include ongoing noise, constant social demands, unpredictable routines, limited escape options, or repeated exposure to triggers without relief.

Over time, chronic stress changes how dogs respond to the world. Their tolerance shortens. Their reactions become faster. Their ability to cope quietly erodes.

A dog living under chronic stress is not "badly trained." They are overloaded.

Stress does not reset overnight

One of the most common misunderstandings about stress is the belief that once a stressful event has passed, the dog has "moved on."

In reality, stress lingers in the nervous system.

Stress hormones do not instantly disappear when a situation ends. If another stressor occurs before the body has fully recovered, the load compounds. This is known as **stress stacking**, and it plays a central role in behaviour escalation.

A dog may cope with:

- a disrupted routine
- a noisy visitor
- a busy outing

But when these events happen close together - or repeatedly - the dog's capacity is gradually depleted.

When behaviour finally escalates, the last trigger is often blamed. But it is rarely the true cause. It is simply the final weight placed on an already overloaded system.

Why stress looks different in every dog

Stress does not have a single presentation.

Some dogs externalise stress. They bark, lunge, pace, vocalise, or react visibly. These dogs are often identified early because their behaviour disrupts human expectations.

Other dogs internalise stress. They withdraw, freeze, hide, shut down, or become unusually quiet. These dogs are often praised for being "easy" or "well behaved."

But silence is not the absence of stress.

A dog who freezes or disengages may be overwhelmed rather than relaxed. A dog who tolerates discomfort quietly may be carrying significant emotional load.

Both expressions of stress are valid. Both deserve attention.

Stress changes how dogs learn

When stress levels rise, the brain shifts priorities.

Survival takes precedence over learning.

In a stressed state:

- impulse control decreases
- memory access weakens
- problem-solving capacity drops

- familiar cues suddenly fail

This is why dogs may appear to "know better" in calm moments, yet struggle completely under pressure. It is not refusal. It is not defiance. It is a biological limitation.

Expecting reliable learning from a stressed nervous system is unrealistic. Training cannot override stress - it must work alongside regulation.

Hidden sources of stress in everyday life

Many sources of stress are not dramatic or obvious. They are woven into daily life and often go unrecognised.

Common hidden stressors include:

- busy households with little quiet time
- constant interaction without rest
- unpredictable schedules
- lack of safe retreat spaces
- emotional upheaval in the home
- social pressure from people or other dogs

None of these indicate poor ownership. But without awareness and adjustment, they accumulate.

Dogs are remarkably adaptive - until they are not.

Why reducing stress changes behaviour faster than training

Many owners are surprised when behaviour improves after environmental or routine changes, even before formal training begins.

This happens because reducing stress restores capacity.

When stress decreases:

- thresholds rise
- recovery improves
- communication softens
- learning becomes accessible again

Training builds skills.
Stress reduction creates the conditions for those skills to work.

Without addressing stress, training efforts are often fragile and inconsistent.

Listening for stress signals

Learning to recognise stress early allows owners to intervene before behaviour escalates.

Early stress signals may include:

- subtle avoidance
- changes in movement
- increased vigilance
- restlessness
- difficulty settling
- reduced tolerance

These signals are not failures. They are information.

Dogs communicate stress long before behaviour becomes unsafe. When owners learn to listen at this stage, outcomes change dramatically.

A Real Life Moment

A dog living in a unit complex began barking persistently.

The barking wasn't constant during the day. It showed up most intensely at night and in the early morning - at footsteps in the hallway, doors closing, neighbours moving about, sounds without a clear source. Complaints began to come in. The situation quickly felt urgent.

His owner was doing everything she could think of. She walked him more, tried to interrupt the barking, and stayed constantly alert for the next sound that might set him off. The home became tense. Sleep was broken. Everyone felt on edge.

The barking was treated as the problem.

What was actually happening was overload.

The dog lived in an environment where sound, movement, and proximity were constant and unpredictable. During the day, his nervous system worked hard to cope - processing noise, activity, and expectation without much opportunity to fully disengage. By night, his capacity was gone.

The barking wasn't about alerting. It was about a nervous system that hadn't had enough recovery.

What helped wasn't teaching him to be quiet, it was being aware of how much his body was being asked to manage.

Reducing what his body was being asked to manage meant quieter evenings, fewer expectations once he was tired, and prioritising rest before overload set in. With less pressure to cope, his nervous system settled - and the barking eased as a result.

Evenings became deliberately quieter. Demands were lowered. Rest was protected instead of postponed. The goal shifted from "getting through the day" to allowing his nervous system to settle before it reached its limit.

As recovery improved, the barking reduced.

Not completely. Not immediately.

But enough that sleep returned, tension eased, and the household stopped bracing for the next eruption.

The change didn't come from control, but from relief.

A question that reframes behaviour

Instead of asking:
"Why is my dog doing this?"

Ask:
"What pressure is my dog under right now?"

That question shifts the focus from control to understanding. It invites curiosity rather than frustration. And it opens the door to meaningful change.

Looking ahead

In the next chapter, we'll explore one of the most misunderstood concepts in dog behaviour: the difference between tolerance and calm - and why mistaking one for the other can have serious consequences.

Stress is not a weakness.
It is a signal.

When we learn to recognise it, behaviour stops feeling unpredictable - and starts making sense.

Chapter 3:
Tolerance Is Not The Same As Calm

One of the most common - and most dangerous - misunderstandings in dog behaviour is the belief that a dog who is quiet, compliant, or still must be calm.

They aren't growling.
They aren't barking.
They aren't resisting.

So they must be fine.

But calm and compliant are not the same thing.

And mistaking tolerance for calm is one of the primary reasons stress goes unnoticed until it escalates into behaviour that feels sudden, extreme, or out of character.

What tolerance actually is

Tolerance is a coping strategy.

It is what happens when a dog endures a situation they find uncomfortable, frightening, or overwhelming because they do not feel able to escape, communicate more clearly, or change the outcome.

A tolerant dog is not relaxed.
They are managing.

Tolerance often develops in dogs who learn that subtle communication is ignored, ineffective, or discouraged. Over time, these dogs stop trying to express discomfort early and instead endure situations quietly.

From the outside, this looks like a well-behaved dog.

From the inside, it is often anything but.

Why tolerance is so easily missed

Tolerance does not disrupt human expectations.

A tolerant dog:

- stays still
- remains quiet
- allows handling
- does not challenge

Because nothing appears "wrong," discomfort goes unnoticed. In busy households, tolerant behaviour is often praised. Dogs are described as easy, gentle, or good with everyone.

But tolerance is not an emotional state.
It is a survival strategy.

And survival strategies have limits.

Calm is a regulated state, not stillness

True calm comes from nervous system regulation.

A calm dog shows flexibility - not rigidity. They are able to engage and disengage, to approach and retreat, to rest and move with ease.

Calm dogs:

- move freely
- show soft, loose body language
- make choices
- recover quickly after stress
- re-engage voluntarily

Calm includes curiosity and agency.

Tolerance does not.

A tolerant dog often appears still because movement feels unsafe or pointless. They may remain in place not because they are relaxed, but because freezing is the safest option available.

The freeze response and shutdown

When dogs experience sustained pressure without escape, they may enter a freeze response.

Freeze is often misunderstood as calm because it lacks obvious movement. In reality, freeze is a high-stress survival state where the body becomes still to avoid drawing attention or escalating conflict.

Over time, repeated freezing can lead to shutdown.

Shutdown dogs may appear:

- unusually quiet
- disconnected
- withdrawn
- compliant without engagement

These dogs are often praised for being "easy" or "low maintenance," when in reality, they are overwhelmed.

Shutdown is not emotional wellbeing.
It is exhaustion.

Why tolerant dogs are often the ones who "snap"

When tolerant dogs finally reach their limit, the behaviour that follows often shocks everyone.

"There were no warning signs."
"He's never done anything like this before."
"She just snapped."

But warning signs were almost always present - they were simply subtle, quiet, or misunderstood.

Tolerance delays escalation; it does not prevent it.

When coping strategies collapse, behaviour intensifies rapidly because the dog has learned that earlier communication did not work.

How we accidentally teach tolerance

Most tolerance is not created through cruelty or neglect. It develops through misunderstanding and well-intentioned expectations.

Dogs are often expected to tolerate:

- hugging
- constant handling
- close face-to-face interaction
- forced greetings
- busy environments
- lack of personal space

When dogs endure these situations without overt protest, the behaviour is repeated. Over time, dogs learn that discomfort must be endured quietly.

This learning does not build resilience.
It builds suppression.

The cost of chronic tolerance

Living in a state of ongoing tolerance is emotionally and physically draining.

Dogs managing chronic tolerance may:

- struggle to settle
- become hypervigilant
- show sudden reactivity
- withdraw from interaction
- display changes in appetite or sleep
- lose interest in play

These changes are often attributed to personality or age, rather than recognised as signs of stress accumulation.

Tolerance masks distress until it can no longer be sustained.

Choice is the difference between calm and tolerance

One of the clearest ways to distinguish calm from tolerance is the presence of choice.

A dog who is calm:

- can move away freely
- can disengage without consequence
- returns voluntarily
- initiates interaction

A dog who is tolerating:

- stays because escape feels unsafe
- avoids eye contact
- shows subtle tension
- does not re-engage willingly

Choice reduces pressure.
Pressure removes choice.

When dogs are given agency, tolerance is no longer necessary.

Why This Matters for Safety

From a safety perspective, tolerance is unreliable.

Dogs who feel able to communicate early rarely escalate. Dogs who feel trapped often do.

Recognising tolerance early allows owners to intervene before behaviour becomes risky. It protects dogs from being pushed beyond capacity and protects people from unexpected escalation.

Safety improves when communication is respected.

A shift in how we assess "good behaviour"

Instead of asking:
"Is my dog behaving?"

Ask:
"Is my dog comfortable?"

Comfort creates stability.
Stability creates predictability.
Predictability creates safety.

Behaviour that comes from comfort is far more reliable than behaviour that comes from endurance.

Looking ahead

In the next chapter, we will examine why punishment and suppression fail dogs - and how attempts to stop behaviour often remove the very signals that keep everyone safe.

Tolerance keeps the peace temporarily.
Calm sustains it.

Understanding the difference changes everything.

Part II:
Why Behaviour Escalates

Behaviour does not escalate randomly. It escalates when pressure accumulates, communication fails, and coping strategies collapse.

This section examines the mechanisms behind escalation - including punishment, nervous system overload, and environmental pressure - and explains why well-intentioned approaches so often make things worse.

Chapter 4:
Why Punishment Fails Dogs

Punishment is often used because it appears to work.

The behaviour stops.
The moment passes.
Control feels restored.

From the outside, it can look like success.

But stopping behaviour is not the same as helping a dog feel safe - and safety is what determines whether behaviour improves or escalates over time.

Punishment does not resolve the emotional state driving behaviour. It suppresses expression. And when expression is suppressed without addressing cause, the underlying stress remains.

What punishment actually teaches

Punishment does not teach dogs what *to* do.

It teaches them what *not* to express.

When a dog is punished for growling, barking, avoiding, or snapping, the lesson learned is not calm or understanding. The lesson is that communication is unsafe.

The dog still feels uncomfortable.
The dog still feels threatened.
The dog still needs relief.

But now, they are less likely to warn.

This is how dogs become quiet - and unsafe.

Fear and learning cannot coexist

When a dog is frightened, their nervous system prioritises survival.

In this state:

- the thinking brain becomes less accessible
- memory retrieval weakens
- impulse control drops
- learning capacity shuts down

Punishment applied during fear does not teach understanding. It compounds stress and increases urgency.

A dog cannot learn safety through fear.

This is not philosophy - it is biology.

Why punishment creates "good" dogs - temporarily

Many dogs subjected to punishment appear to improve at first.

They comply more quickly.
They hesitate before reacting.
They suppress visible signs of distress.

This is often mistaken for learning.

But what has actually changed is risk assessment. The dog is no longer deciding what feels safe - they are calculating consequences.

This is not calm.
It is vigilance.

Vigilant dogs may comply, but they are not emotionally regulated. Over time, vigilance is exhausting.

The loss of warning signals

One of the most serious consequences of punishment is the loss of early warning signals.

Growling, avoidance, stiffening, and disengagement are not failures - they are protective communication. When these signals are punished, dogs learn to skip them.

The result is a dog who appears fine - until they are not.

Most serious incidents are not caused by dogs who "never warned."
They are caused by dogs whose warnings were ignored or punished.

Why punishment escalates behaviour over time

Punishment often leads to escalation because it adds stress to an already stressed system.

As stress accumulates:

- thresholds lower
- reactions become faster
- recovery takes longer

- tolerance collapses

Owners may respond by increasing intensity, believing they need to be firmer. This creates a feedback loop where fear and pressure intensify together.

What looks like defiance is often desperation.

The illusion of control

Punishment can create the illusion of control.

The dog stays still.
The behaviour stops.
Compliance increases.

But control is not trust.

Dogs who behave out of fear are not choosing cooperation. They are avoiding consequences. This is a fragile state - one that depends on constant pressure to maintain.

When pressure slips, behaviour returns.

Why suppression is risky

Suppressed behaviour does not disappear. It goes underground.

Dogs still feel discomfort.
They still experience stress.
They still need relief.

But without safe communication, escalation becomes the only option left.

This is why punishment-based approaches often lead to sudden, severe reactions after long periods of apparent calm.

What actually helps instead

Effective behaviour change focuses on:

- reducing stress
- increasing predictability
- managing environments
- teaching alternative coping strategies
- supporting regulation

This does not mean permissiveness. It means effectiveness.

When dogs feel safe enough to communicate, behaviour becomes clearer, earlier, and easier to manage.

A safer question to ask

Instead of asking:
"How do I stop this?"

Ask:
"What is my dog trying to achieve by behaving this way?"

That question opens the door to solutions that reduce behaviour rather than suppress it.

Looking ahead

In the next chapter, we'll explore the nervous system itself - and why regulation must come before learning if behaviour change is going to last.

Punishment may stop behaviour.
Understanding changes it.

Chapter 5:
The Nervous System Comes First

Before behaviour can change, before learning can occur, and before training can be effective, one thing must be in place: regulation.

Dogs do not choose behaviour in isolation. Every response they offer is filtered through their nervous system - a system whose primary job is survival. When a dog feels safe, learning and connection are possible. When a dog feels threatened or overwhelmed, survival takes priority.

This is not a choice.
It is biology.

Understanding the nervous system changes how we interpret behaviour. It shifts the question from "Why won't my dog do this?" to "Is my dog capable of coping right now?"

What the nervous system is constantly doing

A dog's nervous system is always scanning the environment, asking one central question:

Am I safe?

If the answer is yes, the body relaxes. Heart rate steadies, muscles soften, digestion functions normally, and the brain is available for learning and problem-solving.

If the answer is no, the body prepares for survival. Hormones are released, perception narrows, and behaviour shifts toward protection.

Dogs do not reason their way into these states. They enter them automatically, based on perception - not logic.

This is why a dog can be "fine" one moment and completely unable to cope the next. The nervous system has shifted gears.

The survival responses: Fight, flight, and freeze

When a dog's nervous system perceives threat or overwhelm, it activates one of three primary survival responses.

Fight responses include growling, snapping, lunging, barking, or guarding behaviour. These are attempts to create distance or stop a perceived threat.

Flight responses include fleeing, hiding, avoidance, pulling away, or refusing to engage. These behaviours are attempts to escape pressure.

Freeze responses include stillness, shutdown, dissociation, or compliance without engagement. Freeze is often misunderstood as calm because it lacks movement, but it is a high-stress state.

All three responses are normal. None indicate a bad dog. They indicate a nervous system under pressure.

Why learning shuts down under stress

When the nervous system enters survival mode, the brain reallocates resources.

Thinking becomes secondary.
Memory access reduces.
Impulse control weakens.

This is why dogs may appear to "forget" training under stress. They haven't forgotten - their brain simply isn't available to access those skills.

Expecting reliable learning in this state is unrealistic. It is similar to asking someone in a panic to follow complex instructions. The body is not ready.

Training does not override the nervous system.
It must work with it.

Regulation is not obedience

One of the most common misunderstandings is confusing regulation with compliance.

A regulated dog is not necessarily still or quiet. Regulation looks like:

- loose, fluid movement
- soft facial expression
- ability to disengage and re-engage
- curiosity
- recovery after stress

A dysregulated dog may appear obedient, especially if they have learned that movement or expression brings consequences. But obedience without regulation is fragile.

True regulation allows flexibility.
Dysregulation creates rigidity.

How chronic stress alters the nervous system

When dogs live under ongoing stress, their nervous system adapts - but not in a healthy way.

Chronic stress can lead to:

- heightened vigilance
- lowered thresholds
- faster escalation
- slower recovery
- reduced tolerance

These dogs are not "on edge" by choice. Their nervous system has learned that the world is unpredictable and requires constant monitoring.

Behaviour becomes reactive not because the dog wants to react, but because their baseline state has shifted.

Why calm must come before training

Many owners attempt to train their way out of stress.

They add more cues, more repetition, more correction - believing consistency will eventually solve the problem.

But training relies on a nervous system that is regulated enough to learn.

This is why behaviour often improves when:

- environments are simplified
- routines are stabilised
- pressure is reduced
- rest is protected

Regulation creates capacity.
Capacity allows learning.

Without regulation, skills collapse under pressure.

Supporting regulation in everyday life

Supporting a dog's nervous system does not require advanced techniques. It requires awareness and consistency.

Helpful supports include:

- predictable routines
- safe retreat spaces
- adequate sleep and rest
- reduced social pressure
- sniffing and foraging activities
- calm, low-demand interaction
- appropriate physical exercise

These are not optional extras. They are biological needs.

Dogs who regularly meet these needs cope better with stress, recover faster, and learn more reliably.

Why regulation takes time

Nervous systems do not reset instantly.

Dogs who have lived with chronic stress may need time before calm becomes accessible. Progress often appears subtle:

- shorter reactions
- quicker recovery
- softer communication
- increased willingness to engage

This is not stagnation.
It is healing.

Expecting rapid change places pressure on the very system you are trying to support.

A question that changes expectations

Instead of asking:
"Why won't my dog behave?"

Ask:
"Is my dog regulated enough to cope with this right now?"

That question prevents unrealistic expectations and protects dogs from being pushed beyond capacity.

Looking ahead

In the next chapter, we'll explore how environment shapes behaviour - and why changing surroundings often creates faster, more reliable change than training alone.

The nervous system is the foundation beneath every behaviour.

When we support it first, everything else becomes possible.

Chapter 6:
Environment Matters
More Than You Think

When behaviour changes, most people instinctively look at the dog.

What's wrong with him?
Why is she suddenly doing this?
Has something changed in their training?

But behaviour rarely begins *inside* the dog. More often, it begins around them.

Environment is one of the most powerful influences on behaviour - and one of the most underestimated. Dogs are constantly responding to their surroundings: physical space, noise, movement, routines, emotional tone, and social expectations. Change any one of these, and behaviour often shifts with it.

Sometimes dramatically.

What "environment" really includes

When people hear the word environment, they often think only of location - the house, the yard, the park.

But environment is broader than place. It includes everything a dog experiences moment to moment, such as:

- physical space and layout
- noise levels and unpredictability
- routines and timing
- number of people or animals present
- emotional tension in the household
- access to rest and retreat
- social expectations and pressure

A dog may cope well in one environment and struggle in another, not because they are inconsistent, but because the demands placed on them are different.

Why new environments are so demanding

New environments require enormous emotional effort.

Unfamiliar smells, sounds, movement, and expectations all place demand on the nervous system. Even environments that appear enjoyable - busy parks, social gatherings, daycare settings - can be overwhelming, especially for dogs already carrying stress.

In these situations, dogs are often expected to cope without sufficient support, rest, or choice. When behaviour escalates, the environment is blamed last - even though it is often the primary driver.

A dog who struggles outside the home is not failing. They are responding to increased load.

The problem with "they'll get used to it"

One of the most persistent myths in dog behaviour is the belief that repeated exposure automatically builds confidence.

Sometimes it does.

Often, it doesn't.

Exposure without safety, choice, and recovery does not build resilience. It builds sensitisation - where dogs become more reactive over time rather than less.

Confidence develops when dogs feel safe enough to process experiences, not when they are forced to endure them repeatedly.

A REAL LIFE MOMENT

Two dogs had lived together peacefully for years.

There had never been a fight. No obvious guarding. No dramatic incidents. From the outside, the home appeared calm and well balanced.

Over time, one dog began to change.

He became restless, easily startled, and irritable in situations that had never bothered him before. He struggled to settle and reacted sharply to interruptions. His guardian was confused - nothing obvious had changed, and the dogs still appeared to get along.

There was no conflict to point to. Only constant proximity.

In shared spaces, one dog always yielded. He moved aside first, waited longer, rested lightly, and remained alert even during downtime. He never complained. He simply adapted.

For years.

The behaviour that eventually surfaced wasn't sudden. It was the result of long-term social effort without relief. His nervous system had been negotiating space constantly, without ever fully resting.

When opportunities for separation were introduced - quiet time alone, predictable breaks from shared space - his behaviour began to soften. Not because the relationship was repaired, but because the pressure was reduced.

Nothing about the dogs' relationship had been "wrong." But one of them had been carrying more than was visible.

Peaceful coexistence requires ongoing effort - and effort has limits.

Busy homes and invisible pressure

Some of the most stressful environments are loving, busy homes.

Multiple people.
Multiple animals.
Constant interaction.
Little uninterrupted rest.

None of this is malicious. But without intentional boundaries, pressure accumulates.

Dogs in busy homes often have limited opportunities to disengage. They are expected to be available - to tolerate handling, noise, movement, and proximity - for long periods.

Over time, even the most tolerant dogs may struggle.

Emotional environment matters

Dogs are highly attuned to emotional tone.

Grief, illness, anxiety, conflict, and exhaustion all shape the emotional environment of a home. Dogs notice changes in body language, routine, energy, and interaction patterns - even when humans try to hide them.

Behaviour changes following emotional upheaval are not coincidence. They are communication.

Dogs do not need words to understand that something has shifted.

Small changes, big impact

One of the most hopeful truths about behaviour is that small environmental changes often produce significant improvement.

These changes may include:

- adding a quiet retreat space
- adjusting routines
- reducing social pressure
- managing access to stimulating areas
- separating dogs during high-arousal moments
- protecting rest

These are not dramatic interventions. They are practical adjustments that lower baseline stress and restore capacity.

When environment improves, behaviour often follows.

Why management is not failure

Many owners resist management because it feels like admitting defeat.

Using gates, leads, separation, structured routines, or controlled access is sometimes viewed as giving in - as though a "good" dog shouldn't need these supports.

But management is not failure.
It is responsibility.

Management prevents escalation while capacity is rebuilt. It protects dogs from being placed in situations they are not equipped to handle yet.

Ignoring the need for management often creates the very behaviour owners hope to avoid.

Changing environment before changing behaviour

One of the most effective approaches to behaviour change is addressing environment *before* addressing training.

When environment supports the dog:

- stress decreases
- thresholds rise
- communication softens
- learning becomes possible

Training layered on top of a supportive environment is far more effective than training used to compensate for environmental overload.

A question that shifts perspective

Instead of asking:
"How do I fix my dog?"

Ask:
"What in my dog's environment is making this harder than it needs to be?"

That question moves responsibility where it belongs - not as blame, but as opportunity.

Looking ahead

In the next chapter, we'll explore how life changes - grief, illness, age, and upheaval - reshape behaviour, and why expecting dogs to stay the same through change is unrealistic.

Environment is not background noise.

It is an active force shaping behaviour every day.

Part III:
Life, Ethics & Responsibility

Dogs do not live in controlled environments or static circumstances. They live alongside us - through change, loss, growth, and complexity.

This section explores the ethical responsibilities that come with that reality, including social pressure, consent, and the impact of life changes on behaviour.

Chapter 7:
When Life Changes, Dogs Change

Dogs are often described as adaptable, resilient, and forgiving.

And in many ways, they are.

But resilience does not mean immunity. Dogs experience the world through routine, predictability, and emotional safety. When those foundations shift, behaviour often shifts with them - sometimes quietly, sometimes dramatically.

Dogs do not need to understand change to be affected by it. They feel it in their bodies, their routines, and their relationships. When life changes, behaviour is often the first place those changes appear.

Change is stress - even when it's positive

Stress is not reserved for fear, trauma, or obvious disruption. Change itself is stressful, even when it is welcomed or beneficial.

A new baby.
A new partner.
A move to a new home.
A change in work hours.
A new animal in the household.

From a human perspective, these changes may be planned, rational, and positive. From a dog's perspective, they are simply different. Different requires adjustment, and adjustment requires emotional effort.

When multiple changes occur close together, or when support does not increase alongside change, coping capacity can quickly be exceeded.

Grief in dogs is real

Dogs form deep attachments - to people, to other animals, and to familiar patterns of life. When a companion is lost through death, separation, or absence, dogs notice.

They may not understand the concept of death, but they understand that someone is missing.

Grief in dogs may look like:

- withdrawal or clinginess
- searching behaviour
- changes in sleep or appetite
- lowered tolerance
- increased anxiety
- regression in behaviour

Some dogs become quiet and subdued. Others become restless or reactive. Both responses are normal.

Grief does not follow a timetable. Dogs process loss at their own pace, and their behaviour during this time reflects confusion, adjustment, and emotional strain.

Behaviour after loss is often misunderstood

When behaviour changes after loss, owners are often caught off guard.

A dog who was previously tolerant may suddenly growl.
A calm dog may begin to hide.

A confident dog may seem unsettled or unpredictable.

These changes are sometimes described as "acting out." In reality, they are signs of a nervous system struggling to recalibrate in a world that no longer feels the same.

Loss lowers thresholds.
Stress tolerance shrinks.
Coping strategies weaken.

Dogs experiencing grief need safety, consistency, and reduced pressure - not correction.

A REAL LIFE MOMENT

A woman reached out to me, just a few weeks after her husband had passed away suddenly.

There were two dogs in the home. One had belonged primarily to her husband. The other was hers.

What confused her most was that the husband's dog showed no noticeable change at all. He continued with his routines, rested easily, and did not appear distressed. In contrast, her own dog changed dramatically.

He became fearful and reactive. He began hiding under the bed and growling whenever she or her fifteen-year-old son tried to approach or speak to him. He refused interaction and seemed unreachable. The behaviour was frightening and felt completely out of character.

The owner couldn't understand it. She was still there. Her husband's dog was coping. Why wasn't her dog?

The difference wasn't attachment to the person who had died - it was sensitivity to the emotional environment around him.

Her husband's dog did not know he wasn't coming back. From his perspective, a familiar person was temporarily absent. Life, though changed, was still predictable.

Her dog, however, was deeply attuned to her. He sensed the grief, the shock, the emotional disorientation. The person who anchored his sense of safety was still physically present - but internally, everything had changed.

His nervous system went into overdrive.

He did not understand what was wrong. He only knew that the world no longer felt safe.

When I asked whether he had ever used the space under the bed before, the answer came easily. As a puppy, he had often hidden his toys there. It had always been a place of retreat - familiar, enclosed, predictable. Under the bed wasn't avoidance. It was self-protection.

When pressure was reduced - when he was given space rather than coaxed, approached, or corrected - his nervous system began to settle. Nothing was demanded of him. His need for safety was respected.

One evening, only a few days after our initial conversation, and without prompting, he came out into the lounge room. He carried a toy from under the bed and placed it beside his owner's leg. Then he lay down and fell asleep there.

Nothing had been trained.

The dog had simply found his way back when his body felt safe enough to do so.

Seen in context, his behaviour was not a problem to solve, but a response to a world that had changed.

Illness, pain, and ageing

Physical change is another major driver of behavioural shifts.

Pain, discomfort, and age-related decline alter how dogs experience the world. Even low-level, chronic pain can reduce tolerance and increase reactivity.

A dog who once enjoyed handling may now avoid it.
A dog who coped with noise may now startle more easily.
A dog who was patient may become irritable.

These changes are often misinterpreted as attitude or stubbornness. But behaviour is frequently the first sign that something physical has changed.

When behaviour shifts, health should always be part of the conversation.

Emotional climate matters

Dogs are deeply sensitive to emotional tone.

Grief, anxiety, conflict, exhaustion, and stress in the household do not go unnoticed. Even when routines remain largely the same, emotional shifts can change how safe and predictable the world feels.

Dogs may respond by:

- becoming more vigilant
- seeking reassurance
- withdrawing
- struggling with separation
- showing changes in behaviour that seem unrelated

This is not manipulation.
It is attunement.

Dogs live in emotional context as much as physical one.

Why expectations often need to change too

One of the hardest parts of supporting dogs through life changes is adjusting expectations.

Owners often say:
"He used to be fine with this."
"She's never had a problem before."

These statements are understandable - but they assume dogs remain static through change.

They don't.

Supporting dogs during change often means:

- lowering demands temporarily
- simplifying routines
- reducing social pressure
- allowing regression without punishment
- offering more rest and predictability

This is not going backwards.
It is meeting the dog where they are.

Healing is rarely linear

Recovery from change does not happen in a straight line.

There will be days where behaviour improves, followed by days that feel like setbacks. This fluctuation is normal. It reflects a nervous system testing safety, adjusting, and rebuilding capacity.

Progress may appear subtle:

- shorter reactions
- quicker recovery
- increased willingness to engage
- softer communication

These signs matter, even when behaviour is not yet stable.

When change unmasks underlying stress

Sometimes life changes do not *create* new issues - they expose existing ones.

A dog who was coping at the edge of capacity may no longer manage once additional stress is introduced. Behaviour that was previously suppressed may surface.

This does not mean the dog has "changed personality."
It means their coping strategies are no longer sufficient.

Supporting dogs through change

Support during life changes is less about doing more and more about doing *less* - with intention.

Helpful support often includes:

- maintaining predictable routines
- protecting rest and sleep
- reducing expectations
- providing safe retreat spaces
- avoiding unnecessary exposure to stressors
- offering calm, low-pressure interaction

Presence matters more than performance.

A question that grounds perspective

Instead of asking:
"Why is my dog doing this now?"

Ask:
"What has changed in my dog's world?"

That question invites compassion rather than frustration. It reframes behaviour as response, not failure.

Looking ahead

In the next chapter, we'll explore how living with multiple dogs changes behaviour dynamics - and why social pressure in multi-dog homes is often underestimated.

Change does not break dogs.

Unrecognised pressure does.

When dogs are supported through change, behaviour stabilises - and trust deepens.

Chapter 8:
Multi-Dog Homes & Social Pressure

Living with more than one dog is often imagined as companionship multiplied.

More play.
More comfort.
More enrichment.

And sometimes, that is true.

But multi-dog homes are not simply single-dog homes with extra bodies. They are complex social systems, shaped by space, resources, individual coping styles, and emotional pressure. When multiple dogs live together, owners are no longer managing individual behaviour alone - they are managing relationships.

And relationships carry pressure.

Why multi-dog homes are different

Every additional dog changes the environment.

Each dog brings their own:

- stress thresholds
- communication style
- coping strategies
- learning history
- emotional needs

Even dogs who are generally social may struggle when proximity is constant and choice is limited. Unlike dogs who meet in neutral spaces, dogs living together do not choose when to interact, when to disengage, or how much space they have.

Coexistence is often a requirement - not a preference.

Tolerance is often mistaken for harmony

One of the most common assumptions in multi-dog homes is that lack of conflict equals wellbeing.

"They get along."
"They've never fought."
"They're fine together."

But absence of conflict does not necessarily mean absence of stress.

Dogs may tolerate constant proximity because avoiding conflict feels safer than expressing discomfort. Subtle signals are often missed, especially when dogs are quiet or compliant.

Tolerance can look like harmony - until it collapses.

Social pressure builds quietly

Social pressure rarely announces itself.

It builds through:

- limited personal space
- constant proximity
- competition for attention
- unpredictable movement
- lack of retreat options

Dogs may cope for months or years without overt conflict. But coping is not the same as thriving.

When pressure accumulates without relief, thresholds lower. Behaviour that once seemed stable becomes fragile. Incidents that appear sudden often have long histories of quiet stress behind them.

The myth of "pack"

The idea of the domestic dog pack is often romanticised.

In reality, dogs living together are not a natural pack. They are a group assembled by circumstance, not choice. They did not select their companions, their space, or their routines.

This does not mean dogs cannot live happily together. It means that harmony requires intentional management - not assumption.

Dogs should not be expected to "work it out themselves" when power imbalances, stress, or resource pressure exist.

Resource pressure is not always obvious

When people think of resources, they often think only of food or toys.

But resources also include:

- human attention
- resting places
- doorways and movement paths

- proximity to owners
- predictability and routine

Tension around these resources may be subtle. Dogs may block access, hover, withdraw, or monitor each other without overt aggression.

These behaviours are often missed or dismissed - until pressure escalates.

Why longevity does not equal safety

Many serious incidents in multi-dog homes occur between dogs who have lived together peacefully for years.

"They've been together forever."
"They've never had a problem."

Time does not guarantee stability.

Dogs change. Stress accumulates. Health shifts. Tolerance decreases. What was once manageable may no longer be.

Past harmony does not ensure future safety.

The impact of change in multi-dog homes

Changes that affect one dog often affect the entire group.

Illness.
Ageing.
Injury.
Loss.
Emotional upheaval.

When one dog's behaviour changes, social dynamics shift. Dogs may become more vigilant, less tolerant, or more reactive.

Multi-dog homes are especially vulnerable during periods of change, because pressure increases while capacity decreases.

Why management protects relationships

Management in multi-dog homes is often misunderstood as failure.

Separating dogs.
Rotating access.
Feeding separately.
Using gates or crates.

These strategies are not signs of defeat. They are signs of responsibility.

Management reduces pressure, preserves communication, and prevents escalation. It allows dogs to coexist safely without forcing constant interaction.

The goal is not togetherness at all costs.
The goal is sustainable safety.

When social pressure turns into conflict

Conflict is most likely during:

high-arousal moments

disruptions to routine

competition for attention

illness or pain

emotional household stress

These moments lower tolerance and increase risk - especially when dogs are already managing underlying pressure.

Early intervention matters.

A hard but necessary truth

Not all dogs are suited to live together without support.

This does not mean anyone has failed.
It means reality has shifted.

Safety must come before sentiment.

Protecting dogs sometimes requires difficult decisions, but avoidance of those decisions often carries far greater cost.

A question that reframes multi-dog behaviour

Instead of asking:
"Why did this happen?"

Ask:
"What pressure has been building here for a long time?"

That question invites prevention rather than blame.

Looking ahead

In the next chapter, we'll explore the role of choice and consent - and why allowing dogs to opt out is one of the most powerful safety tools available.

Multi-dog homes do not fail because dogs are bad.

They struggle when pressure goes unrecognised.

Chapter 9:
Choice, Consent & Safety

Safety does not come from control alone.

It comes from understanding, predictability, and the ability to step away before pressure becomes overwhelming. One of the most effective - and most misunderstood - ways to achieve this is through choice and consent.

For some people, these ideas feel abstract or impractical. There is concern that allowing dogs choice will lead to chaos, disobedience, or a lack of boundaries. In reality, the opposite is true.

Choice and consent are not indulgences.
They are safety mechanisms.

What consent means for dogs

Dogs cannot give consent verbally, but they communicate it clearly through behaviour.

Consent is shown through:

- voluntary approach

- relaxed, loose body language
- willingness to stay engaged
- ability to disengage freely
- returning by choice after moving away

Consent is not a one-time agreement. It is ongoing and changeable. A dog who is comfortable in one moment may not be comfortable the next - and that shift matters.

A dog who feels able to opt out does not need to escalate.

Why "they let me" is not the same as consent

One of the most common and dangerous misunderstandings in dog ownership is the belief that tolerance equals agreement.

A dog may allow:

- hugging
- close face-to-face contact
- grooming or handling
- interactions with children
- social greetings

But allowing something because escape feels unsafe is not consent.

Stillness is not permission.
Freezing is not comfort.
Endurance is not calm.

Dogs who feel trapped may remain still because movement could escalate the situation. This is not cooperation - it is self-preservation.

Choice reduces pressure

When dogs are given choice, pressure decreases.

Choice allows dogs to:

- regulate their own comfort
- communicate early
- disengage before stress escalates
- return voluntarily when ready

Dogs who trust that their signals will be respected do not need to shout to be heard. Their communication remains subtle, early, and safe.

Removing choice increases pressure.
Increasing pressure increases risk.

Where choice matters most

Choice is especially important in situations that carry emotional or physical vulnerability, including:

- handling and grooming
- interactions with children
- greetings with unfamiliar people or dogs
- confined spaces
- new environments
- periods of illness, pain, or stress

In these contexts, forced compliance may appear efficient, but it creates long-term instability.

Safety is not built through endurance.

Boundaries create safety - not force

Choice does not mean a lack of structure.

Dogs can have clear boundaries, predictable routines, and guidance without being forced to tolerate discomfort. Structure and consent are not opposites - they work together.

Healthy boundaries:

- prevent overwhelm
- protect communication
- reduce conflict
- create predictability

Force silences communication.
Boundaries support it.

Children, dogs, and adult responsibility

Children do not intuitively understand dog body language. They rely on adults to guide safe interaction.

It is not reasonable - or safe - to expect dogs to tolerate:

- constant handling
- unpredictable movement
- loud emotional expression
- lack of space

Teaching children to respect a dog's "no" builds empathy and prevents harm. It also protects dogs from being placed in impossible situations.

A dog should never be responsible for managing a child's behaviour.

Off-lead culture and forced interaction

Many dogs experience significant social pressure in public spaces where choice is limited or removed entirely.

Off-lead greetings, crowding, and assumptions of friendliness often place dogs in positions where avoidance is impossible. Even social dogs may struggle when interaction is unavoidable.

A dog who avoids interaction is not rude.
A dog who needs space is not aggressive.

Advocating for a dog's space is not overprotective - it is responsible.

Why ignoring consent escalates behaviour

When dogs learn that subtle communication is ignored, they escalate.

They move from:

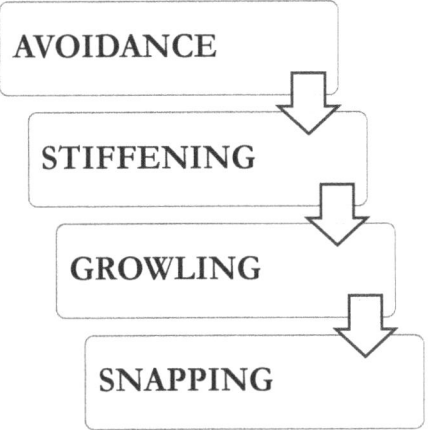

This progression is not sudden. It is learned.

Escalation occurs when early signals fail.

Dogs do not become dangerous because they communicate - they become dangerous when communication is ineffective.

Choice does not mean chaos

Allowing choice does not remove leadership, guidance, or structure.

Dogs can be guided while still being allowed to:

- move away
- say no
- disengage safely

Structure without choice creates compliance. Structure with choice creates trust.

Trust creates reliability.

Consent as a safety lens

Viewing behaviour through a consent lens changes everyday decisions.

Instead of asking:
"How do I make my dog do this?"

Ask:
"Does my dog feel safe enough to choose this?"

That question prevents countless incidents - not by lowering standards, but by aligning expectations with capacity.

When choice is limited

There are times when choice must be limited for safety - veterinary care, emergencies, or necessary handling.

In these moments, safety is increased when:

- stress is minimised where possible
- handling is calm and predictable
- recovery and decompression follow

Temporary limitation of choice is safest when it is the exception, not the rule.

Looking ahead

In the next chapter, we move from understanding into action - exploring what helping actually looks like in everyday life, and how small, consistent decisions create meaningful change.

Choice is not permissiveness.

It is prevention.

Part IV:
Action & Support

Understanding behaviour matters, but understanding alone is not enough.

This final section focuses on what helping actually looks like in real life - how to support dogs practically, when to ask for help, and how to make decisions that protect both safety and relationship.

Chapter 10:
What Helping Actually Looks Like

When people talk about helping dogs with behaviour, the image that often comes to mind is intervention during crisis.

The moment of the growl.
The lunge that scares someone.
The incident that forces action.

But real help rarely begins in crisis. In fact, the most effective help usually happens quietly, long before behaviour becomes confronting.

Helping is not louder, firmer, or faster.
It is earlier, calmer, and more intentional.

Helping starts with seeing patterns, not isolated moments

Behaviour is rarely random.

What often looks like unpredictability is actually pattern we haven't learned to see yet. Helping begins when owners stop focusing on single incidents and start paying attention to what happens around them.

Patterns often emerge in:

- specific times of day
- particular environments
- moments of transition
- periods of fatigue or excitement
- interactions with certain people or dogs

Once patterns are recognised, intervention becomes preventative rather than reactive.

Helping starts with observation - not correction.

Helping often means reducing, not adding

When behaviour becomes challenging, many owners instinctively add more:

- more training
- more rules
- more structure
- more correction

But many dogs are already overloaded.

In these cases, adding more demands increases pressure and reduces capacity. Helping often means doing less - intentionally.

This may include:

- simplifying routines
- lowering expectations temporarily
- reducing social exposure
- shortening outings
- limiting stimulation

Reducing pressure does not reward behaviour. It supports recovery.

Helping is management - and that's a good thing

Management is one of the most effective - and most misunderstood - forms of help.

Using gates, leads, separation, crates, or controlled access is often viewed as failure, as though a well-adjusted dog should not need these supports.

In reality, management is foresight.

Management:

- prevents rehearsal of unwanted behaviour
- protects dogs from overwhelm
- keeps people safe
- creates space for learning later

Without management, dogs are repeatedly placed in situations they cannot cope with, and behaviour becomes entrenched.

Helping means advocating, even when it's uncomfortable

Helping a dog often requires advocating on their behalf - especially in social settings.

This may mean:

- declining greetings
- asking people to give space
- preventing unwanted handling
- stepping in before tension escalates

Advocacy is not rudeness.
It is responsibility.

When dogs learn that someone will intervene for them, their need to escalate decreases. Trust builds not through force, but through protection.

Helping happens in the nervous system first

Behaviour change does not start with obedience. It starts with regulation.

Helping looks like:

- protecting rest and sleep
- ensuring dogs have retreat spaces
- maintaining predictable routines
- allowing decompression after stress
- supporting regulation before training

A dog that is regulated can learn. A dog who is overwhelmed cannot.

Helping respects this order.

Helping includes teaching skills - at the right time

Training absolutely has a place in helping dogs. But timing matters.

Skills are best taught when:

- stress levels are manageable
- environments are supportive
- expectations match capacity

Teaching a dog what *to* do works best after pressure has been reduced - not while the dog is already struggling to cope.

Helping is meeting the dog where they are, not where we wish they were.

Helping is allowing rest without guilt

Many dogs live overstimulated lives.

Busy households, frequent outings, constant interaction, and little uninterrupted rest place enormous demand on the nervous system.

Helping may look like:

- fewer activities
- shorter social interactions
- more quiet time
- protected sleep

Rest is not laziness.
It is biological maintenance.

Dogs who rest well cope better with everything else.

Helping is consistency, not perfection

Helping does not require flawless execution.

It requires:

- consistency over time
- willingness to adjust
- honesty about limits
- patience with progress

There will be days when behaviour improves and days when it doesn't. Helping is staying steady through both.

Progress is rarely linear - and that is normal.

Helping sometimes means letting go of expectations

One of the hardest parts of helping is releasing expectations that no longer serve the dog.

This may include:

- letting go of social ideals
- adjusting plans
- redefining success
- accepting current limitations

Letting go is not giving up.
It is adapting.

Helping respects the dog's reality, not an imagined version of who they "should" be.

Helping is a relationship, not a technique

The most important thing to remember is this:

Dogs do not need perfect owners.
They need responsive ones.

Helping is built through daily decisions - not dramatic interventions. It is quieter than people expect and slower than people want.

But it works.

A question that grounds action

Instead of asking:
"What should I do right now?"

Ask:
"What would make this moment easier for my dog to cope with?"

That question leads to safer, calmer decisions - every time.

Looking ahead

In the next chapter, we'll talk about when to seek additional support - and how asking for help protects dogs, owners, and relationships.

Helping is not about fixing dogs.

It is about supporting them.

Chapter 11:
When To Ask For Help

Most people wait too long before asking for help with their dog.

Not because they don't care - but because they believe they should be able to handle it themselves. They worry about being judged, about being told they've failed, or about hearing advice that feels harsh, outdated, or unsafe.

So they wait.

They manage quietly.
They minimise concerns.
They hope things will improve on their own.

Sometimes they do. Often, they don't.

And waiting can make everything harder than it needs to be.

The myth of "I should be able to fix this"

There is a strong cultural narrative around dog ownership that suggests good owners should cope without help.

That seeking support means:

- you've done something wrong
- you've missed obvious signs
- you're not capable enough

This belief keeps people silent - even when behaviour is escalating or safety feels uncertain.

But behaviour challenges are rarely the result of one mistake or one decision. They develop through layers of stress, environment, learning history, and emotional capacity. Many of these factors are outside an owner's control.

Needing help is not failure.
It is awareness.

When support becomes important

Support is especially important when behaviour begins to feel unmanageable or unsafe.

This may include:

- escalation in intensity or frequency
- growling progressing to snapping or biting
- fear dominating daily routines
- management no longer feeling sufficient
- constant vigilance in the household
- owners feeling anxious, exhausted, or overwhelmed

These are not signs you've waited too long - they are signs that extra support would help.

Trust the feeling when something doesn't feel right.

Safety is a valid reason to ask for help

One of the most important things to understand is that safety alone is reason enough to seek support.

You do not need to justify concern.
You do not need to wait for an incident.
You do not need to reach crisis point.

Protecting people and animals is responsible ownership.

Dogs do not benefit from being pushed past capacity, and people do not benefit from living in fear or constant stress.

What ethical help looks like

Not all behaviour support is equal.

Ethical, effective support should:

- prioritise safety and wellbeing
- avoid fear, intimidation, or punishment
- consider stress, environment, and emotional state
- work at a realistic pace
- support owners without shame

Good support feels collaborative, not corrective. It should help you understand your dog - not fear them.

If support feels dismissive, rushed, or coercive, it is okay to seek another option.

Why earlier is better

The earlier support is sought, the more options exist.

Early intervention:

- prevents escalation
- preserves communication
- reduces risk
- protects relationships
- improves outcomes

Waiting rarely makes behaviour easier to change. It often makes it more complex.

Seeking help early is not overreacting - it is preventative care.

You don't have to be at breaking point

Support does not have to be a last resort.

Sometimes, one conversation provides clarity.
Sometimes, reassurance is all that's needed.
Sometimes, a small adjustment changes everything.

Help is not only for crisis.
It is also for understanding.

Asking for help helps everyone

When owners feel supported, they make clearer decisions.

When stress decreases in the household, dogs cope better.

When guidance is available, fear loses its grip.

Asking for help protects:

- dogs
- people
- relationships
- quality of life

It is an act of care - not defeat.

A question that opens the door

Instead of asking:
"Is this bad enough to need help?"

Ask:
"Would support make this safer, clearer, or easier?"

If the answer is yes, reach out.

Looking ahead

In the final pages of this book, we'll bring everything together - not with rules or pressure, but with perspective, understanding, and trust.

Conclusion: Listening Changes Everything

Dogs are not difficult.

They are expressive, adaptive beings navigating a world built for humans - a world that often expects far more of them than we realise.

Throughout this book, we have explored how behaviour is shaped by stress, environment, emotional capacity, life changes, social pressure, and the nervous system itself. We have examined why tolerance is mistaken for calm, why punishment silences communication, and why choice and consent are essential for safety.

The common thread through all of it is this:

Behaviour makes sense when we understand the context.

Calm is built, not demanded

Calm does not come from stricter rules, louder voices, or greater control.

It comes from:

- safety
- predictability
- reduced pressure
- choice
- early intervention

Calm grows when dogs feel heard rather than managed. It becomes accessible when nervous systems are supported rather than pushed.

This process is rarely quick - but it is reliable.

Understanding changes outcomes

When owners shift from reacting to behaviour to responding to need, everything changes.

Behaviour becomes clearer.
Escalation becomes preventable.
Relationships become safer.

Understanding does not excuse unsafe behaviour - it prevents it.

You do not need to be perfect

This book was never meant to create pressure.

You will make mistakes.
You will misread moments.
Life will interrupt your best intentions.

That does not undo the relationship you are building.

Dogs do not need perfect owners.
They need present, responsive ones.

Earlier listening creates safer lives

Dogs who are listened to early do not need to escalate.

Owners who understand behaviour do not need to rely on force.

Households that prioritise safety do not need to live in fear.

Listening earlier changes outcomes - quietly, steadily, and profoundly.

The most important truth

If you take only one thing from this book, let it be this:

When a dog struggles, they are not being difficult. They are communicating.

And when we learn to listen, everything changes.

In closing

Understanding is the most powerful training tool we have.

Behaviour is not static, and neither is understanding. As dogs age, as life changes, and as circumstances shift, behaviour will continue to evolve. The skills in this book are not meant to be mastered once and set aside - they are meant to be returned to, refined, and adapted over time. Listening is not a one-time act. It is an ongoing relationship.

Acknowledgements

This book exists because of many people, animals, and experiences that shaped how I see dogs and behaviour.

First, to the dogs - past and present - who taught me far more than any qualification ever could. Every dog I've lived with, trained, observed, and learned from has contributed to the understanding woven through these pages.

To my aunty, Joy Parker, whose influence on my understanding of dogs cannot be overstated. Through her lifelong dedication to breeding Australian champions across many breeds, including the careful importing and exporting of bloodlines, she developed an exceptional understanding of dogs built on sound conformation and stable, functional temperaments. Her deep knowledge of structure, behaviour, and breed purpose - and her generosity in sharing that knowledge - shaped the foundations of how I learned to truly see dogs.

My aunty taught me to watch interactions, notice subtle shifts, and recognise when pressure was building - lessons that shaped how I read dogs far more deeply than any textbook ever could.

Joy found people hard to get along with, and they rarely understood her, but she understood dogs in a way few ever do. She could tell you what a dog was thinking long before anyone else noticed a change - reading tension, intent, and emotion with extraordinary clarity.

Looking back, I realise was one of the few people who truly understood her. I believe now that was because we shared the same gift - an ability to listen to animals, and to value what they were communicating over what was expected of them. Joy was never concerned with how she was perceived by people; she cared only about what the animals thought of her.

To those who have asked for my advice, trusted it, and then taken the brave step of acting on it with your own dogs - thank you. Many of you have thanked me over the years, but I want you to know that I thank you. Thank you for allowing me into your lives, your homes, and your relationships with your dogs. Thank you for being willing to look at things in a different way, try something new, and put understanding ahead of judgement. Being able to make a genuine difference in your lives has been an honour.

To the clients who trusted me with their dogs and their stories - your honesty, vulnerability, and willingness to look beyond labels continues to inform my work more than you know.

To my family, for supporting a life deeply entwined with animals, learning, and advocacy - thank you for the patience, understanding, and belief that allowed this work to exist.

And finally, to the readers: if this book helped you pause, listen differently, or feel less alone in your experience with your dog, then it has done exactly what it was meant to do.

About The Author

Amy Curran holds a Diploma in Animal Psychology and is the author of the bestselling book *Your First Puppy: A Guide for Children*. She holds multiple professional accreditations across animal behaviour, training, performance, and assessment, and has spent her life working alongside animals in a wide range of settings.

Amy has bred and shown Australian Cattle Dogs to CACIB, State, and Royal level, and is the owner and trainer of Bernie (Malicloy Five O'Clock Somewhere), the first and only Bernese Mountain Dog in the world to achieve the highest level of

Animal Actor Certification with the International Academy of Animal Actors. She has trained many animals for film, television, and commercial work, including dogs, cats, and horses, and is known for her ability to work across species while respecting individual capacity, communication styles, and emotional wellbeing.

Amy is also the trainer of the Norwegian Forest Cat Sylvester (Fairwind Black Opal), who was awarded the title of Australia's Most Talented Cat. Working with Sylvester allowed her to deepen her understanding of feline behaviour and further develop her specialist knowledge of multi-species relationships.

Amy breeds Heritage Australian Stock Horses, focusing on sound conformation and temperament, and her children actively ride, train, and learn alongside them.

Amy is the founder of a Young Horse Trainers Program, the first initiative of its kind to place completely unhandled yearling ponies into the hands of child trainers aged between 10 and 16. These ponies, bred by long-term friend April Moulds-Dumbleton, provided young handlers with a rare opportunity to learn how to read behaviour, build trust, and develop ethical training skills from the very beginning. The program reflects Amy's long-standing commitment to sharing knowledge and teaching others how to understand animals, rather than simply manage them.

She is also the founder of the Animal Talent Academy of Australia, an organisation dedicated to ethical, positive, and relationship-centred animal training and assessment. Amy is a Certified Assessor with the Academy, a Certified Canine Fitness Coach, a Certified Trick Dog Instructor, and an Animal Actor Assessor with Do More With Your Dog (USA). During COVID, Amy was ranked the Number 1 Trick Dog Trainer in Australia and Number 6 worldwide.

Amy advocates for a calm, ethical approach to training - one that prioritises understanding, safety, and emotional wellbeing over labels and quick fixes.

Through years of working across species, Amy has become a specialist in multi-species relationships, focusing on how animals of different species learn, communicate, and live together in harmony, while keeping respect for each animal as an individual.

www.ingramcontent.com/pod-product-compliance
Lightning Source LLC
Chambersburg PA
CBHW062037290426
44109CB00026B/2649